GEARED FOR GROWTH BIBLE STUDIES
LORD, TEACH US TO PRAY
A STUDY ON PRAYER

BIBLE STUDIES TO IMPACT THE LIVES
OF ORDINARY PEOPLE

Written by Shirley Andrews

The Word Worldwide

CHRISTIAN
FOCUS

Scripture quotations marked (ESV) are taken from *The Holy Bible, English Standard Version*, copyright © 2001 by Crossway Bibles, a publishing ministry of Good News Publishers. Used by permission. All rights reserved. ESV Text Edition: 2011.

Scripture quotations marked (NASB) are taken from the *New American Standard Bible*®, Copyright © 1960, 1962, 1963, 1968, 1971, 1972, 1973, 1975, 1977, 1995 by The Lockman Foundation Used by permission. (www.lockman.org)

Scripture quotations marked (GNT) are taken from the *Good News Translation in Today's English Version – Second Edition* Copyright © 1992 by American Bible Society. Used by permission.

Scripture quotations marked (KJV) are taken from the *King James Version*.

For details of our titles visit us on our website
www.christianfocus.com

ISBN 978-1-78191-969-9

Copyright © WEC International

Published in 2017
by
Christian Focus Publications Ltd.,
Geanies House, Fearn, Ross-shire,
IV20 1TW, Scotland, UK,
and
WEC International, Bulstrode, Oxford Road,
Gerrards Cross, Bucks, SL9 8SZ.

Cover design by Alister MacInnes

Printed in the UK by Bell & Bain, Glasgow.

CONTENTS

PREFACE 4
INTRODUCTORY STUDY 5

QUESTIONS AND NOTES

STUDY 1 – PRAYER IS CONVERSATION WITH OUR HEAVENLY FATHER 7
STUDY 2 – WHAT PRAYER CAN DO FOR YOU 10
STUDY 3 – PRAYER IN THE CHURCH RELEASES THE POWER OF GOD 13
STUDY 4 – CHURCH LIFE AND GROWTH RESULTS FROM PRAYER 16
STUDY 5 – PRAYER BRINGS VICTORY 19
STUDY 6 – BEGIN PRAYER WITH PRAISE 22
STUDY 7 – PRAYER IS THANKSGIVING AND CONFESSION 25
STUDY 8 – PRAYER IS INTERCESSION AND SUPPLICATION 28
STUDY 9 – CONDITIONS FOR PRAYER... 31
STUDY 10 – MORE CONDITIONS FOR PRAYER 34
STUDY 11 – TYPES OF PRAYER 37
STUDY 12 – THE PRAYER LIFE OF JESUS 40

ANSWER GUIDE

STUDY 1 44
STUDY 2 45
STUDY 3 46
STUDY 4 47
STUDY 5 48
STUDY 6 49
STUDY 7 50
STUDY 8 51
STUDY 9 52
STUDY 10 53
STUDY 11 54
STUDY 12 55

PREFACE
GEARED FOR GROWTH

Where there's LIFE there's GROWTH:
Where there's GROWTH there's LIFE.

WHY GROW a study group?
Because as we study and share the Bible together we can

- learn to combat loneliness, depression, staleness, frustration and other problems
- get to understand and love each other
- become responsive to the Holy Spirit's dealing and obedient to God's Word

and that's GROWTH.

How do you GROW a study group?

- Just by asking a friend to join you and then aim at expanding your group
- Study the set portions daily (they are brief and easy: no catches)
- Meet once a week to discuss what you find
- Befriend others, both Christians and non-Christians, and work away together

see how it GROWS!

WHEN you GROW ...

This will happen at school, at home, at work, in your youth group, your student fellowship, women's meetings, mid-week meetings, churches and communities, and so on.

you'll be REACHING THROUGH TEACHING

WHEN you PRAY ...

Remember those involved in the writing and production of the study courses: pray for missionaries and nationals working on the translations into many different languages. Pray for groups studying that each member will not only be enriched personally, but will be reaching out continually to involve others. Pray for group leaders and those who direct the studies locally, nationally and internationally.

WHEN you PRAY ... Realise that all profits from sales of studies go to develop the ministry on our mission fields and beyond, pay translators, and so on, and have the joy of knowing you are working together with them in the task.

INTRODUCTORY STUDY

In the next twelve weeks in our study together we plan to learn from the Lord on the subject of 'Prayer'. He will speak to us about prayer in our personal prayer life, in family life and in our church fellowship.

At the beginning it is good for us to see what the New Testament says about the place of prayer in the lives of the followers of Jesus.

SCRIPTURES TO CONSIDER
What is the Lord telling us to do?

Luke 18:1
Luke 21:36
Romans 12:12
Ephesians 6:18
Colossians 4:2
1 Thessalonians 5:16-18
Jude 20

Perhaps for some of us prayer is something fairly new. But for all of us there are usually things we find difficult about prayer.

GROUP EXERCISE
Do we find prayer easy?

Make a list of the difficulties you have with prayer. Share these.

Keep the list and during the weeks of study pray about these difficulties and see what the Lord says about them.

The title for this study is in itself a request. The disciples of Jesus had been with Him as He prayed. They too wanted to learn to pray. So they asked, 'Lord, teach us to pray.'

Read Luke 11:1-13
How did Jesus respond to their request?

Consider their request, 'Lord, teach us to pray.' They could have asked, 'Lord, teach us all about prayer.' Do you see any difference in these two requests?

What encouragement to pray does Jesus give His disciples? (vv. 9, 10, 13).

Jesus recognises and responds to our desire to pray.

We can liken learning to pray to a child learning to ride his new bicycle. He could prepare an excellent project on the way bicycles are constructed, or give a talk on the advantages of being a cyclist, while the bicycle remains in the garage. There comes a day when he must get on and ride, maybe in a very wobbly way, but he has to put theory into action!

'Though a man have all knowledge about prayer, and although he understands all mysteries about prayer, unless he prays, he will never learn to pray.'

The Path of Prayer – Chadwick

Paul says in 1 Corinthians 8:1 'Knowledge puffs up.' Our study is not designed for us just to acquire knowledge, but that the knowledge becomes practice in our lives.

OUR AIM in this study is that we **all** become better pray-ers.

A personal question to answer:

What do you want the Lord to do for you as we study?

....

....

....

....

Turn that into a prayer and write it below.

....

....

....

....

....

Spend time together in prayer, sharing your individual prayers. Maybe you wish to echo the request of Jesus' disciples:

'LORD, TEACH US TO PRAY.'

STUDY 1
PRAYER IS CONVERSATION WITH OUR HEAVENLY FATHER

QUESTIONS

DAY 1 When God created Adam and Eve they had unbroken communion with God. But one day they rebelled against Him and that fellowship was shattered.
Genesis 3:8-13.
When the Lord God came to Adam and Eve what did they do?

How did God respond to their silence?

What followed between God and Adam and Eve?

DAY 2 Abraham's nephew, Lot, chose to live in Sodom. God told Abraham of His plan to destroy Sodom because of its sinful state.
Genesis 18:22-33.
Abraham asked God questions. How did God respond?

What followed between God and Abraham?

DAY 3 In Jesus, God has done all to put us in a right relationship with Himself.
Romans 10:12-13; Luke 23:40-43.
What does man have to do to be put right with God?

On the cross, what did the dying thief do?

What was the result?

DAY 4 As we believe in the Lord Jesus Christ we have a whole new relationship with God.
Ephesians 1:3-6; Ephesians 2:18.

QUESTIONS (contd)

DAY 5 *James 4:8 (a)*
What is God's gracious invitation and promise to us?

John 16:23-27.
What does Jesus tell us about the Father?

The Father's promise to answer prayer in verse 23 is linked with verse 27. To whom is the promise made?

DAY 6 The Old Testament people of God had a time of cruel slavery in Egypt. They cried to their God for help.
Exodus 2:23-25; 3:7-8.
That cry brought results. Write at least five things that God did.

DAY 7 *Psalm 34:1-4, 15-17; Psalm 55:16-17.*
What does God do for His people?

What does David tell us about God's readiness to listen?

NOTES

The Westminster Shorter Catechism asks, 'What is the chief end of man?' And the answer is, 'Man's chief end is to glorify God, and to enjoy Him for ever.' The Lord made us to have a relationship with Him as Father. We saw that this relationship was broken when Adam and Eve rebelled. But God provided a way back. Jesus is 'the Way' to the Father. Through Jesus we have access to the Father (John 14:6).

Prayer is the amazing privilege of the children of the Father. He, the Living, Eternal God of all the earth, invites His children to draw near to Him.

Prayer is conversation with our Heavenly Father. If prayer is conversation with our Heavenly Father, do we need to use big words, a special tone of voice, or special theological language?

As we saw on the second day when we read about Abraham, prayer means speaking to God and listening to Him. Speaking and listening are the two necessary parts of all conversation.

Questions to think about

Do I expect God to speak to me?

Is it good prayer if I speak to God and do all the talking?

How well do I listen to Him?

Jesus tells his followers 'always to pray' (Luke 18:1). But prayer is never meant to be a drudge or a burden.

'There is no greater joy on earth or Heaven than communion with God, and prayer in the name of Jesus brings us into communion with Him. The Psalmist was surely not speaking only of future blessedness when he said, "In Thy presence is fullness of joy" (Ps. 16:11). O the unutterable moments when in our prayers we really press into the presence of God!'

How to pray – R. A. Torrey.

STUDY 2
WHAT PRAYER CAN DO FOR YOU

QUESTIONS

DAY 1 *Hebrews 4:14-16.*
Because of Jesus what does God tell us to do?

In what manner are we to come before the Father in prayer?

What are the two gifts we receive?

DAY 2 *John 16:23-24.*
As well as answers to prayer what else do we receive?

Here is one of the secrets of being joyful. What is it?

Have you been filled with joy by the Father answering a specific prayer?

Share it in your group.

DAY 3 *Psalm 10:14; Philippians 4:6-7.*
What does the verse from Psalm 10 tell us about the Father and our troubles?

Underline and think about the 'anything' and 'everything' in Philippians 4:6. Is there a cure for anxiety?

DAY 4 *Psalm 55:22; 1 Peter 5:6-7.*
How does the Father want us to deal with our troubles?

Psalm 37:5
What two things are we to do, and what is the Father's promise to us?

QUESTIONS (contd)

DAY 5 *James 1:5-6.*
How does God give? How are we to ask? What does He give?

Discuss the importance of awareness of need relative to praying.

DAY 6 *Psalm 138:3; Psalm 34:4.*
What other gifts does the Father give as we pray?

Psalm 34: 6, 17, 19.
What is the secret of dealing with the fears that cripple us?

DAY 7 *Matthew 6:11; Luke 11:9-13.*
What are we to ask for and why is this meant to be a daily prayer?

What wonderful gift is the Heavenly Father prepared to give and to whom is He given?

NOTES

Look back over your notes and complete the chart.

By prayer, we receive

Hebrews 4:16 ....

John 16:24 ....

Philippians 4:6-7 ....

James 1:5 ....

Psalm 138:3 ....

Psalm 34:4 ....

Psalm 34:17 ....

Matthew 6:11 ....

Luke 11:13 ....

Do you need any or all of the above gifts? We receive them all by prayer.

What a privilege the Father has given His children! We may come boldly to Him through Jesus. The Father pours blessing into our lives as we pray. God answers our prayers. Our God is real to us. He is with us. Our hearts are thrilled by Him.

> 'O what peace we often forfeit.
> O what needless pain we bear.
> All because we do not carry
> Everything to God in prayer.'

Is this true in your life?

Who is holding the burdens and cares of your life right now?

STUDY 3
PRAYER IN THE CHURCH RELEASES THE POWER OF GOD

QUESTIONS

DAY 1 *Acts 1:4-5.*
What did Jesus tell his disciples to do?

What did Jesus promise would happen to them?

Acts 1:14
What does Acts 1:14 tell us about unity in a praying group?

DAY 2 The disciples were obedient. They stayed in Jerusalem and prayed. *Acts 2:1-6.* What did God do?

Acts 2:32-33. What led to the fulfilment of Acts 1:4-5?

DAY 3 *Acts 2:42; 4:31; 12:5; 16:25.*
What do these verses tell us about the early Church?

The infant Church faced problems as it grew, *Acts 6:1-4.* What choice did the leaders make?

DAY 4 In Acts 3 Peter and John healed a lame man. A great crowd gathered and 5,000 men believed. So Peter and John were arrested and told not to teach in the name of Jesus.

Acts 4:23-31.
What two things did the believers ask the Lord to do?

What did the Lord do about their first request?

QUESTIONS (contd)

Acts 5:12-16.
How did the Lord answer their second request?

DAY 5 *Acts 5:17-21*
How did the Lord continue answering the prayer?

NO PRAYER = NO POWER. What do you think?

DAY 6 *Acts 12:1-11.*
What did King Herod do to the Church?

What did the Church do?

How did God respond?

DAY 7 *Acts 12:12-17.*
What did Peter find the believers doing?

How do you think those people felt as they heard Peter's story?

NOTES

According to John chapter 3, we are born of the Spirit. He produces fruit in our lives – Galatians 5:22-23. He gives spiritual gifts and equips us for ministry – 1 Corinthians 12. But the Father gives the Holy Spirit to those who ask Him.

The early disciples devoted themselves to prayer. The Father poured out on them the gift of His Holy Spirit. Those early disciples saw the power of prayer.

There was commitment in the early church – commitment to the Gospel and mission, commitment to one another and commitment to prayer as a group.

There is a place for personal, private prayer.

But the early Church also prayed as a group. Prayer released the power of God in their lives. Prayer released the power of God in their ministry. Prayer produced miracles.

Questions to think about

In the Christian group of which you are a part, how do you measure up with the early Church in this matter of group or corporate prayer?

Are you a praying people?

Pause for Prayer:

Talk to the Father about your spiritual needs.

Bring the spiritual needs of your Church fellowship before Him.

How about asking for boldness to talk to others about Jesus.

Maybe you and your Church need to ask God to show His power among you.

STUDY 4
CHURCH LIFE AND GROWTH RESULTS FROM PRAYER

QUESTIONS

DAY 1 *Colossians 1:18; Matthew 16:18.*
What do these verses tell us about the Church?

What does the head do for a physical body?

What do you expect Jesus, the Head, wants to do for His body?

DAY 2 *Acts 13:1-4*
As they were worshipping, what did God do?

What did the Church do?

Was Paul's first great missionary journey begun as a result of men planning or men praying?

DAY 3 In prayer the Lord reveals His plans and strategies to His people. *Jeremiah 33:3* (a good verse to memorise).
What is God's command and what two things does He promise to do?

Have you ever had the experience of the Lord revealing things to you as you prayed?

DAY 4 *Acts 6:7; 9:31; 12:24; 16:5; 19:20.*
What important feature of the early Church is described in these verses?

List the ways in which there was growth in the Church.

QUESTIONS (contd)

DAY 5 In the Church you attend do you see people growing in the Word? In faith? In discipling others? In witnessing? And is the Church growing numerically?

DAY 6 *James 4:2*
Write this important principle in your own words.

Could this be a word for you?

Is your Church fellowship aware of, and responsive to, such areas of need?

DAY 7 *Romans 1:9; Ephesians 1:16; Colossians 1:3, 9;
1 Thessalonians 1:2; 2 Timothy 1:3.*
What do these verses tell us about Paul – the first great missionary?

NOTES

As we have seen this week, strategies and plans were revealed as the early Church prayed. They were all of one mind. In a congregation the Lord won't tell two men one plan and two others something entirely different. In a case like this, someone isn't listening. The Lord has only one mind.

Corporate, or group prayer was a priority in the life of the New Testament Church. Amazing growth resulted. Prayer is the key to Church life and growth today.

All through history, times of growth and times of repentance and revival have come as a result of prayer.

> 'In the twentieth century, the long-lasting East African Revival was birthed in prayer. Tiredness characterised the Church in Uganda in the 1930s. Church attendance was poor. Worship was dull. African Christians were being pulled away by growing wealth, racial feelings and bad habits.
>
> Blasio spent a week in his hut, praying and meditating.
>
> He returned to put things right at home between himself and his wife, and from that time, Blasio was a man on fire. The fire spread. There were many conversions and Pentecostal outbreaks, with people experiencing dreams and trembling, and having all-night praise meetings.'
>
> *The Church in East Africa.* W.B. Anderson.

As a result, hundreds of thousands of people in Uganda have come to Christ. It all began when one man sought God in prayer.

One man sought God in prayer, got right with God and others. Many leaders of the Church in East Africa today are the fruit of this revival. The blessing 'flowed over' from the Ugandan Church to touch and bless other fellowships and countries.

Pause for prayer

*Pray that we may live with Jesus as Head of our families and congregations.

*Pray for your congregation: Acts 9:31

> to be built up;
> to walk as a Church in the fear of the Lord;
> to walk in the strengthening of the Holy Spirit;
> to grow;

*Pray as above for the whole Church in our nation.

STUDY 5
PRAYER BRINGS VICTORY

QUESTIONS

DAY 1 *1 Peter 5:8; Ephesians 6:10-20.*
Who is the Christian's enemy, and what does he desire?

What does God command us to do?

DAY 2 *Ephesians 6:10-20; John 17:15.*
Write out verse 18. Underline 'all', 'every' and 'always'.

What are we to do, how are we to pray, and for whom?

What did Jesus pray for us?

DAY 3 *John 14:30; 16:11; 2 Corinthians 4:4; Ephesians 6:11.*
What names are given to Satan?

1 John 5:19. Who rules the world?

DAY 4 Genesis shows us that man, when tempted by Satan, chose rebellion against God as a way of life.
By doing this, man gave dominion in the earth to Satan. Evil is on the earth because man chose it to be there. It was never God's plan. But God is just and cannot go back on that which He committed to man.
On the whole, mankind continually chooses in favour of Satan, giving Satan the legal right to be in the earth. And he knows it!

Galatians 4:8; Ephesians 2:1-3.
Why did Jesus come?

John 12:31-32. Would Satan be overthrown?

QUESTIONS (contd)

DAY 5 *Colossians 2:15.*
How does Paul describe the victory Jesus won by His cross?

2 Corinthians 2:14. What is God's purpose for His people?

DAY 6 *James 4:6-10.*
What practical steps could you take to obey these commands and claim the promises? Discuss how you can put Satan to flight.

1 John 4:4; Romans 8:31; Revelation 12:11.
On what basis do we overcome Satan?

DAY 7 *Matthew 4:10.*
What did Jesus tell Satan to do?

Luke 10:19.
What authority did Jesus give to His followers whom He sent out?

1 Peter 5:8-9.
What are we to do to Satan.

NOTES

The Lord makes it plain that Christians are in a battle with the forces of evil. Satan, the enemy of God, plans to thwart and hinder the plans and purposes of God. He tries to hinder and cripple the people of God.

Sometimes Christians fall into two errors as far as Satan is concerned. Both are dangerous. The one is to live without any understanding of Satan and his plans, as if he didn't exist. The other is to be preoccupied with him.

Paul did neither of these things. Look what he wrote to the Corinthian Church:

'For when I forgive – if, indeed, I need to forgive anything – I do it in Christ's presence because of you, in order to keep Satan from getting the upper hand of us, for we know what his plans are.' 2 Corinthians 2:10-11. GNT

Paul knew the enemy, but lived in the light of the victory Jesus won using the weapons of warfare the Lord provides. He was a man of prayer, knowing that prayer brings victory.

Questions to think about

'Christians don't take the battle for the Gospel seriously. The weapon of "all prayer" (Eph. 6:18) is seldom used. Defeat after defeat happens simply because this lesson has not been learned.' Michael Baughen.

- Is this true of your life?
- Is this true of your congregation?

Pause for prayer

*Pray for greater understanding of Christ's victory on the Cross and the victory that is ours. Praise God for this also.

*Pray for a greater effectiveness in spiritual warfare by prayer.

*Jesus gave us His example. When speaking to Peter, Jesus said, "SATAN DEMANDED TO HAVE YOU...BUT I HAVE PRAYED" (Luke 22:31,32 ESV).

For whom should you be praying just as Jesus prayed for Simon?

STUDY 6
BEGIN PRAYER WITH PRAISE

QUESTIONS

DAY 1 Psalm 47:6-7; 59:17; 67:5; 71:5-6.
What was one of the things God's people in the Old Testament were commanded to do?

Psalm 113:1; 150:6; Revelation 19:5.
Who are to praise God, and are you included?

DAY 2 1 Peter 2:4-5.
What does Peter tell Christians to give to God?

Hebrews 13:15-16.
What two sacrifices are Christians to offer to God and how does He receive them?

DAY 3 Psalm 103:1
says, 'BLESS (or praise) THE LORD, O MY SOUL; AND ALL THAT IS WITHIN ME, BLESS HIS HOLY NAME!' (ESV)

Who is to be the focal point of our praise?

From this verse in what measure are we to give ourselves to praise?

"BLESS THE LORD, O MY SOUL." So often in worship we turn this around to "BLESS MY SOUL, O LORD!" If we do this, where is our focus?

DAY 4 Psalm 150:2.
What are the two things for which we are to praise God?

Psalm 147:1-6.
What do you see about praise in verse 1?

QUESTIONS (contd)

In verses 3-5 the Psalmist is praising God for WHO HE IS AND WHAT HE DOES. List these things and praise Him too!

DAY 5 *Psalm 145.*
Find five things about praising God for WHO HE IS.

Find five things about praising God for WHAT HE DOES.

DAY 6 *Psalm 47:1; 68:3-4; 71:22-23; 98:4-6.*
What do these verses tell us of God's people praising Him?

Psalm 33:1-3; 63:3-4; 150.
List the things that may be used to praise God. How many have you seen used in worship.

DAY 7 *Psalm 66:1-2.*
What does the Psalmist tell us about the quality of praise that is due to God?
Describe it in your own words.

Revelation 19:4-8.
What do these verses tell us about praise in heaven?

NOTES

Psalm 100:4
"ENTER HIS GATES WITH THANKSGIVING, AND HIS COURTS WITH PRAISE"
The Temple was the place in which the Lord dwelt. God's people were told to come in the gates with thanksgiving, and go into the courts of the Temple with praise. Today we have access to God our Father through Jesus. But it is a good thing to approach Him with praise and thanksgiving. When we are alone, it is good to begin a time of prayer with praise and thanksgiving. In our family prayers it is good to do this. And in our times of prayer together, it is good to begin with praise and thanksgiving.

PRAISE GETS OUR EYES OFF OURSELVES.
PRAISE GETS OUR EYES OFF OUR CIRCUMSTANCES.
PRAISE LIBERATES!
PRAISE IS THE WAY TO MAKE THE LORD CENTRAL IN OUR PRAYERS AND WORSHIP.

C.S. Lewis, in *Reflections on the Psalms*, writes,

'I had never noticed that all enjoyment spontaneously overflows into praise unless (sometimes even if) shyness or the fear of boring others is deliberately brought in to check it. The world rings with praise…praise of weather, wines, dishes, actors, motors, horses…children, flowers, mountains, rare stamps, rare beetles, even sometimes politicians and scholars. I had not noticed how the humblest, and at the same time most balanced and capacious, minds, praise most…I had not noticed either that just as men spontaneously praise what they value, so they spontaneously urge us to join them in praising it. "Isn't she lovely? Wasn't it glorious? Don't you think that magnificent?" The Psalmists in telling everyone to praise God are doing what all men do when they speak of what they care about.'

Question to think about

'MEN PRAISE WHATEVER THEY VALUE'

What does your 'praise level' tell you about how much you value God?

Pause for prayer

*Spend time daily praising the Lord.

*Pray that God would set you free of the things that hinder praise.

*Pray to learn and experience more of the character of God and the ways of God so that you might praise Him.

STUDY 7
PRAYER IS THANKSGIVING AND CONFESSION

QUESTIONS

DAY 1 *Psalm 50:14-15, 23; 100:2, 4.*
What offering can we bring to God, and how are we to come before Him?

Philippians 4:6; Colossians 2:6-7; 4:2.
What is always meant to be part of our prayers?

DAY 2 *Ephesians 5:19-20.*
We are to give thanks. When? For what? Is this easy to do?

How can you put this into practice?

Colossians 3:15-17.
What is the Lord saying to you about thanksgiving?

DAY 3 *Isaiah 59:1-2.*
What is the Lord's continuing attitude to His people as they pray? But, what happens when we sin?

Psalm 24:3-4; James 4:8.
What do both these passages mention?

What does it mean for you to have 'clean hands and a pure heart'?

DAY 4 *Psalm 66:18; 69:5; Isaiah 1:15; 58:1-10.*
In these verses what does the Lord tell us about sin?

1 John 1:8-9.
What do you have to do in order to be forgiven?

QUESTIONS (contd)

DAY 5 *Psalm 38:18; 51:17; Isaiah 57:15; 2 Corinthians 7:9.*
What attitude does God require in confession?

2 Samuel 24:10, 17.
What did King David experience? Whom did he blame for his sin?

What is to blame for every sin in your life?

DAY 6 *2 Chronicles 7:13-15.*
To whom is the Lord speaking?

What four things does God ask of His people?

What four things does God promise to do if His people obey Him?

DAY 7 *Daniel 9:3-20.*
What did Daniel do? (vv. 3-4).

Whose sin did Daniel confess (verses 5-7, 9-11, 15, 20).

What things did Daniel confess as sin? After confessing the sins of the people (vv. 5-16) what did Daniel begin to do (vv. 17-18).

NOTES

Peter writing to Christians says that God desires them 'to be holy in all your conduct.'

We are to be a 'holy priesthood', 'a holy nation.' (1 Peter 1:15-16; 2:5, 9).

Questions to think about

What attitude do I have towards sin in my life?

Ignore it; Rarely think about it; Feel guilty all the time; Worry about it; Confess it and forsake it; Concentrate on who I am in Christ.

In the light of this week's study, what attitude does the Lord want me to have?

If we are prepared to take sin seriously and deal with it, God promises to forgive, cleanse, blot out and forget our sins (Isa. 43:25). Our prayers, also, will be heard.

The Holy Spirit's work is to convict us of sin.

Have you ever had the experience of a vague, yet heavy sense of being condemned; of being bad and a failure? In Revelation 12:10, Satan is called 'the accuser of our brethren' (NASB). This gives us an insight into what he does. Satan often comes bringing oppressive condemnation to us. It is vague and fuzzy. When the Lord convicts of sin He is specific and encourages us to confession and forgiveness.

Allow the Lord to do the searching. Here is a helpful prayer to pray regularly:

'Search me, O God, and know my heart! Try me and know my thoughts! And see if there be any wicked way in me and lead me in the way everlasting!' (KJV)   *Psalm 139:23-24.*

Our right response is to confess and forsake what He shows us.

Pause for prayer

*Ask God's help to be His thankful child.

*Praise Him that there is a way for sin to be dealt with.

*Pray for right heart attitudes towards sin and God.

*Confess your sin to the Lord.

*Remember to make praise and thanksgiving a part of your daily prayer.

STUDY 8
PRAYER IS INTERCESSION AND SUPPLICATION

QUESTIONS

DAY 1 *1 Timothy 2:1-4.*
In church worship what place should prayer have?
For whom are we to intercede and for what are we to ask?

Numbers 14:11-23.
In his intercession what did Moses talk to God about?

DAY 2 *Daniel 9:1-3, 15-19.*
For whom was Daniel interceding?

What things did he ask God to do? (vv. 17-19).

DAY 3 *Ezekiel 22:23-31* (Verse 30 is a good one to memorise).
Describe the state of God's people in Ezekiel's time.

In this sad mess, what did God look for?

Verse 30 is a good picture of what an intercessor does. Draw a small sketch of what this verse is saying to you.

Because there was no intercessor, what resulted?

DAY 4 *Exodus 32:9-14.*
At this time of national sin, how important was Moses' intercession?

Compare *Psalm 106:23* with *Ezekiel 22:30*. What do you see?

QUESTIONS (contd)

DAY 5 *Philippians 4:6-7.*
Meditate on the Lord's wonderful invitation to us. Write your thoughts. (Think of a child coming to his Daddy with his simple supplication: Daddy please help me fix this...).

God, our heavenly Father, wants us to come as His children freely asking for specific things.

DAY 6 *Luke 11:5-10*
When the man went to his friend, what was his specific request?

How did Jesus end the story?

DAY 7 *Luke 18:35-43.*
What did Jesus ask the blind man?

What was the man's request?

Jesus still asks us the same question. 'WHAT DO YOU WANT ME TO DO FOR YOU?'
Meditate and work out your supplications and take them to Him. (This will not be shared in your group unless you desire).

NOTES

Learn Ezekiel 22:30 by heart.

In that verse we have a picture of a wall broken, leaving a large gap. This allowed for attack and destruction.

An intercessor stands in the breach or gap.

Questions to think about

Think about the walls that protect our nation from the attack of Satan. Do you see them broken in places?

What has broken them down?

What do you think the Lord may be looking for in our land?

We have seen that intercession may be for CITIES, NATIONS, PEOPLES, INDIVIDUALS, IMPORTANT KEY PEOPLE, GOD'S PEOPLE, WORLD LEADERS, ALL MEN.

This gives us wide scope for our intercessions!

Intercession has been described as intensified prayer, and it is, so long as there is emphasis on 'intensified.' In studying Christ and His work of intercession for us, we find three things not necessarily attributed to the general pray-er.

First there is *identification*. Jesus fully identified with us in our sinfulness and 'tasted death' for each of us. He effectively pleads our cause before the Father because He submerged His own desires and gave Himself completely on our behalf. The mark of the true intercessor is that he gives Himself completely on our behalf. The mark of the true intercessor is that he gives himself for the objectives.

Then there is *agony*. It says of the intercessory work of the Holy Spirit, 'He maketh intercession for us with groaning which cannot be uttered.' Through His indwelling, we can likewise become channels of self-giving, agonising intercession for people and a God's Spirit which will strip off carnality, covetousness, self-advancement, etc., and free us, not only for a general part in seeing Christ's Kingdom come on earth, but for specific matters with which the Holy Spirit burdens our hearts.

Lastly there is *authority*. Moses, moving in the authority of God became the 'Saviour' of Israel (physical deliverance out of Egypt into Canaan). Christ, fully accomplishing His Father's will in the finished work of redemption, is exalted to the supreme place of authority on earth and in heaven (Eph. 1:18-23). We, too, can pray in His authority which is what we do when we pray in His will and in the Name (authority) of Jesus.

STUDY 9
CONDITIONS FOR PRAYER

QUESTIONS

DAY 1 *John 15:7-11*
What conditions does Jesus give us to receive 'anything you wish'?

What is involved in 'abiding in Jesus', or 'remaining in Him'?

DAY 2 *Luke 18:9-14*
Describe and contrast the Tax Collector and the Pharisee:
the prayers of the two men;
their attitudes to God themselves and others;
the results of their prayers.

How does *James 4:6* apply to this story and to prayer in general?

DAY 3 *Matthew 6:1, 5-6.*
What important principle does Jesus give us in verse 1?

Where did the hypocrites love to pray? What was wrong with their attitude when they prayed? What reward did they receive?

DAY 4 *James 4:3*
According to this verse, why are some prayers unanswered?

How does God discourage selfishness in His children?

QUESTIONS (contd)

John 14:13; 1 Corinthians 10:31.
What is the true and acceptable motive to have as we pray?

DAY 5 *Psalm 103:2-3, 10, 12; Hebrews 10:17.*
Using these verses, describe God's forgiveness of your sins.

Mark 11:24-25; Matthew 6:12-15.
When we pray, what must we do? Why must we forgive others?

To what degree is your forgiveness by God conditional?

DAY 6 *Mark 11:24-25; Ephesians 4:31-32.*
To what extent and in what manner are we to forgive?
Ask the Lord to show you people whom you have not forgiven. Write down the names. Confess your unforgiving spirit as sin. Pray for them.

DAY 7 *1 John 5:14-15.*
Why is it important to pray according to God's will?

John 5:30; 6:38.
What example did Jesus give us in regard to His own will and the will of the Father?

NOTES

So many of the Lord's promises to us have conditions attached to them. In the Old Testament agreement between God and His people, the Lord promised to give victory, to bless, prosper, increase and keep His people, but this was on condition that they loved, obeyed and worshipped Him (Deut. 11).

So too with the wonderful promises the Lord makes to hear and answer prayer, He sets conditions.

We need to keep these conditions in mind if we want the Lord to hear and answer our prayers. Think about the conditions for prayer we have studied this week:

Questions to think about

        ABIDING IN JESUS   RIGHT MOTIVES

        HUMILITY   FORGIVENESS

RIGHT ATTITUDES   ASKING ACCORDING TO GOD'S WILL

How is your life in regard to these things?

Is there something you could be working on?

Pause for prayer

*Praise and thanksgiving for God's forgiveness and the fact that He makes known His will to us.

*Pray that you and your fellowship or group might learn to walk humbly with God.

*Pray the Father to give you a forgiving spirit. Pray this also for others in your fellowship or group; pray for a setting right of relationships where these have been broken.

STUDY 10
MORE CONDITIONS FOR PRAYER

QUESTIONS

DAY 1 *Ephesians 6:18; Jude 20.*
What condition for prayer do we see in these Scriptures?

1 Corinthians 2:9-13.
What two important truths are we told about the Spirit in verses 10 and 11?

Why do we need to pray in the Spirit?

How does praying in the Spirit tie in with praying according to the will of God?

DAY 2 *James 1:6-8.*
How is a doubter described, and what does doubt do to our prayers?

Matthew 17:20; Matthew 21:18-22.
What condition for prayer did Jesus make plain?

What word did He give His followers about doubt?

What picture did Jesus give of what believing prayer can do?

What 'mountainous' matters is the Lord asking you to pray for, with faith?

DAY 3 *Luke 18:1-8*
What was Jesus' purpose in giving us this parable?

What do we learn from this widow?

QUESTIONS (contd)

DAY 4 *Proverbs 21:13; Malachi 3:8-10.*
What hinders our prayers from being heard?

1 Timothy 6:17-19; Luke 6:38.
How does your Heavenly Father give to you; and how does He want you to give?

DAY 5 *Matthew 18:18-20.*
Who attends every gathering together for prayer, no matter if it is only two or three people?

What does it mean for us to gather together in Jesus' name?

What condition for prayer is given by Jesus in verse 19?

DAY 6 *1 Peter 3:1-7*
What does Peter say can hinder effective prayer?

1 Peter 3:8-12.
What six qualities does Peter tell us we need in verses 8 and 9?
What promise does Peter give us in verse 12, regarding prayer?

DAY 7 *John 14:13-14; 15:16; 16:23-24.*
How does Jesus tell us to ask?

What results from our asking in this way?

NOTES

Jesus came to reconcile us to the Father. Prayer, conversation with the Father, is basic for our ongoing, ever-growing relationship with Him. A basic condition for prayer is that we must be in a continuing right relationship with Him. Meeting the conditions for prayer we have studied flows from a right relationship with Him. Think about them:

ABIDING IN JESUS	PRAYER IN THE SPIRIT
HUMILITY	WITH FAITH
RIGHT ATTITUDES	WITH PERSEVERENCE
RIGHT MOTIVES	GENEROSITY
FORGIVENESS	UNITY
ASKING ACCORDING TO GOD'S WILL	RIGHT RELATIONSHIP IN JESUS' NAME

We need to be continually aware of these conditions the Lord has set for prayer. If our prayers are not being answered, we need to check that we are meeting the Father's conditions for prayer.

In her book, *Something More*, Catherine Marshall writes of a godly visitor in their home sharing with them on this matter.

> 'Well, in my life I've found this forgiveness business a key to getting prayers answered. A couple of years ago I was going through one of those prayers-not-getting-beyond-the ceiling periods and I prayed, "Lord, I don't have enough faith. Give me the gift of faith."
>
> "It isn't your faith," the reply came. "I can see faith even if it's as small as a mustard seed. No, it's something else...When you stand praying – forgive if ye have aught against any. That's your trouble. That's why your prayers aren't answered. You go about with a lot of aughts against a lot of any".'

Questions to think about

'UNITY IS CORPORATE HUMILITY'

What do you think?

Pause for prayer

*Praise the Lord for what He is teaching us.

*Pray that we may not only learn, but *apply* the teaching on conditions for prayer.

*Pray for an increase in your life and in the life of your fellowship of the things Peter lists in 1 Peter 3:8-9.

STUDY 11
TYPES OF PRAYER

QUESTIONS

DAY 1   *Family Prayers: Deuteronomy 4:9-10; 6:4-9.*

What are the Lord's plans for families, or households?

Do you pray on a regular basis in your family?

What are the blessings of a household praying together?

What steps can you take to establish family prayers in your home?

DAY 2   *Personal Prayer: Matthew 6:6-13.*
What is Jesus saying, about personal, private prayer?

Do you sometimes feel overwhelmed by the number of groups and individuals asking for your prayers?

How can you resolve this?

DAY 3   *Prayer with Fasting: Matthew 6:16-18.*
What is fasting and what instructions does Jesus give His followers on this matter?

Daniel 9:1-4; Acts 13:1-3; 14:21-23.
What was the context of the fasting?

Is there a place for fasting today?

DAY 4   Do you find it difficult to pray aloud in a group? Why? Try to list the things that inhibit you like nervousness, shyness, inexperience of group

QUESTIONS (contd)

praying, lack of knowledge of the issues being prayed over, someone else took up 'my' point, etc.

How can you overcome these hindrances and enjoy participating in group prayer?

DAY 5 *Nehemiah 2:1-8.*
What were the circumstances of Nehemiah's quick, pointed 'arrow' prayer?

What do you think Nehemiah may have said to the Lord in his arrow prayer?

What is the value of arrow prayers?

DAY 6 *Prayer for Healing: James 5:14-16.*
What is the sick one to do?

What are the elders to do?

What does the Lord do?

What two things are we to do in order to be healed?

DAY 7 *Prayer for Healing: James 5:14-16; 1 Corinthians 12:4-9.*
Does the Church as a whole act on this word?

What spiritual gift has God given to the Body of Christ to do this work?

Have you yourself experienced healing as James describes, or do you know of someone who has?

NOTES

Question to think about
> Jesus said, 'AND WHEN YOU FAST…'
> Do I?

In Matthew chapter 5 we read that Jesus taught His disciples on three basic related matters, all involved in being a follower of His: Giving, Praying and Fasting.

Jesus assumes we will do all three.

Praying indicates that we are totally dependent on Jesus.

Giving involves bringing ourselves totally into submission to the Lord. It involves bringing our bodily appetites into submission to Jesus. It involves bringing what is legitimate under His control.

While I was preparing the original prayer studies a lady nearby fasted and prayed. The Lord showed her that He wanted to bless and use these studies. Her part was to fast and pray, while I wrote. For almost two years she never told me what she had done. If you have been blessed by them, she certainly had a part in them.

In studying scripture we see there is a link between sin and sickness. Medical science has revealed that physical illness can be caused by certain negative (sinful?) attitudes such as bitterness, resentment, anxiety, fear, unforgiveness, jealousy and smouldering anger. The Spirit of God can convict, cleanse and free the one who repents of such things, often with resultant physical healing.

Read James 5:14-16.

Christians are encouraged to take these verses seriously and literally. Note that the initiative for this kind of praying lies with the individual believer, not with those in positions of leadership. But leaders should be ready and willing to comply! Why is it that not all are healed? Obviously we cannot rule out the fact that the quality of our faith has something to do with it ('the prayer of faith shall save the sick') but it must be conceded that there is a mysterious element here related to the sovereign purposes of God. A. B. Simpson, founder of the Christian and Missionary Alliance – which has healing as one of its main tenets – prayed for many and they were healed, yet he himself had an affliction that remained.

'Some groups believe that verses like Matthew 8:17 and Isaiah 53:4 justify the belief that "healing is in the Atonement". Others feel that this is a misinterpretation and that the Atonement relates purely to the sin question. We recommend that groups avoid trying to handle this problem as it will consume too much of the available time and may possibly create doctrinal division.' (S. R. Dinnen)

Pause for prayer
*Ask for other members of your study group and leader.

*Ask God to help you apply this practical teaching to your life.

STUDY 12
THE PRAYER LIFE OF JESUS

QUESTIONS

DAY 1 *1 Peter 2:21*
What does Peter say about Jesus, and us His followers?

John 6:38; 15:10: 5:19-20; 13:12-16: Philippians 2:5-8.
What four things are said here about Jesus' attitude to His Father?

DAY 2 *John 11:41; Matthew 3:16-17; 17:5.*
How does the John reference relate to the four things we discovered above?

How did God the Father feel about His Son?

DAY 3 Make four columns in your notebook with the headings: Reference? Where Jesus Prayed? When He prayed? The result.
Luke 3:21-22.
Luke 6:12-14.
Mark 1:32-35.
Luke 5:15-16.
Read these references and fill in the other three columns.

DAY 4 As for the third day using these references:
Matthew 14:19-23; Luke 10:17, 21-22; Luke 9:28-31; Luke 11:1.

DAY 5 As for yesterday using these references.
Luke 22:31-34; Luke 22:39-46; Luke 23:34.

QUESTIONS (contd)

DAY 6 *John 17:1-26 and 18:1.*
When did Jesus offer this prayer?

For whom did He pray?

List some of the things for which He prayed.

DAY 7 *Hebrews 5:7-10; Hebrews 7:25.*
What is said here about the prayer life of Jesus?

What have you learned about prayer from the example of Jesus' life?

What is Jesus doing right now for you?

NOTES

In this last week I'd like to share two instances of the Father's answer to prayer.

When we were missionaries in East Africa my husband, Bob, and I were on a teaching safari in a remote area of north-western Kenya. One evening Bob developed a migraine attack. We were due to be teaching next day and people were walking great distances to attend. Bob went into the bathroom to be sick. I followed him. And there the Lord said to me, 'Pray for healing.' Gently I laid hands on Bob's head and asked the Lord to heal him. This I did silently. The Lord said, 'Now tell him what you have done.' His response was a moan and 'Oh no. If I'm sick, the pain in my head feels better.' But there in the bathroom the Lord heard a simple prayer, and answered. Bob got up next day with no migraine, and we taught the many who came that day. That was in 1974, and he has had no migraine since. Praise the Lord!

While I was writing these studies on prayer I lost a valuable antique gold chain which belonged in the family. Carelessly, I left it in a fitting-room in a large department store in Sydney, a city of 3 million people. I reported my loss to the store. Bob and I prayed. We knew the Lord knew where it was. We asked him simply to care for it and restore it to us. A whole month went by with no word at all, but we continued to pray. We assured my parents that it would be returned. They were very sceptical. One day the phone rang. Mary, a Christian, was ringing to tell the story of how she had found it. She said, 'It was amazing, I could not bring myself to try it on.' Her son had urged her not to return it, but she said she was compelled to do so. When I went to visit Mary, what a time of joy we had as we talked together about the faithfulness and goodness of our Father to hear and answer prayer!

What a precious privilege is prayer! It is one of the great privileges of the children of God – twenty-four-hour-a-day access to our Heavenly Father, Who hears and answers prayer!

Question to think about

> The prophet Zechariah spoke this word from the Lord;
> 'I will fill the descendants of David and the other people of
> Jerusalem with the spirit of mercy and the SPIRIT OF PRAYER.'
> Zechariah 12:10 (GNT)

Is this what you want the Lord to do in your life?

If it is, ask and you will receive.

Pause for prayer

That the Lord may do this, also, in the members of your Bible Study group and in your congregation.

ANSWER GUIDE

The following pages contain an Answer Guide. It is recommended that answers to the questions be attempted before turning to this guide. It is only a guide and the answers given should not be treated as exhaustive.

'LORD, TEACH US TO PRAY' – Luke 11:1

Suggestions for Leaders

This course is designed to give Biblical knowledge about prayer and principles to follow. But it is designed chiefly to motivate us to pray and to get us praying more effectively. So ensure there is adequate time for prayer each week. Encourage your group to expect answers from the Lord and get them to share answers to prayer. Aim to include all in the class prayer time; the timid could be asked to prepare simple prayers before class.

Things to remember when praying together

*Keep prayers short and simple, on one or two matters only.

*Speak up.

*Watch habits such as saying 'Lord' or 'Father' at every phrase, and 'just' this and 'just' that.

*Learn to submit to the Holy Spirit. He will time your move from one topic to another.

Some of the questions don't require class discussion time. They are, as it were, stepping stones in teaching a truth. All that is required is that you check that answers are correct. These will be marked with a small * in your Leader's Guide. Also check the 'Questions To Think About' each week. Sometimes these are also helpful for group discussion.

The prophet Zechariah spoke this word from the Lord;
'I will fill the descendants of David and the other people of Jerusalem with the spirit of mercy and THE SPIRIT OF PRAYER.' Zechariah 12:10 (GNT)

*Pray for an outpouring of the SPIRIT OF PRAYER in your life.

*Pray regularly for your group by name, asking the Lord to fill them with the spirit of mercy and the spirit of prayer.

*Pray that the Lord would do this also in the other groups doing these studies.

Whilst there is no specific commentary recommended for use with this study, it would be helpful to have some books on Prayer available for your group to read.

GUIDE TO INTRODUCTORY STUDY

Group Exercise

Make a list of the things the members share and keep it handy for your own prayer and group prayer. Point out answers as the study progresses.

The Personal Question

Some may need help in turning their request into a prayer. Illustrations are helpful, e.g. 'Right now, I'd like help as I don't know what to pray about.' Prayer: 'Father, please teach me how to pray and show me more of what I may bring to you in prayer.' Amen.

ANSWERS TO STUDY 1

PRAYER IS CONVERSATION WITH OUR HEAVENLY FATHER

DAY 1   *They hid from God.
*God came looking for them and called to them.
A time of conversation or dialogue.

DAY 2   God replied with clear, definite answers.
A conversation.

DAY 3   To call on the name of the Lord.
*Ask Jesus to remember him.
A promise that the thief would be with Jesus in Paradise.

DAY 4   Destined, in love, to be God's sons, chosen by God, given every spiritual blessing.
Have access to the Father.

DAY 5   *God invites us to come close to Him. He promises to come close to us.
*The Father loves us. He is prepared to give if we ask.
Those who love Jesus and believe that He came from the Father.

DAY 6   God heard, God remembered His covenant with Abraham, God saw His people, God knew their condition, God acted: 'I have come down to deliver them.'

DAY 7   *The Lord waits for their cry, hears, answers, acts.
God will listen at any time of day or night.

ANSWERS TO STUDY 2

WHAT PRAYER CAN DO FOR YOU

DAY 1   Draw near to the throne of grace – to Him – come into His presence.
With confidence, boldness.
Mercy, grace. Allow group to share what these two gifts mean to them.

DAY 2   *Joy
*The experience of answered specific prayer.

DAY 3   The Father desires to take them into His hands.
To bring everything in prayer, with thanksgiving to God.

DAY 4   To humble ourselves and hand over entirely to Him our burdens and cares.
We are to commit our way to Him and trust Him. He promises then to act.

DAY 5   God gives generously and graciously. We must ask out of a sense of need and in faith. The Lord gives wisdom.
Students may have slightly different answers. If we feel no sense of need, of lack, we tend to trust in ourselves and our resources, and don't ask the Father for His help.

DAY 6   An inner strength. A deliverance from fear.
*Praying about our fears and inner conflicts.
In our troubles, He promises to hear us when we pray, to save us, to *help us, to deliver us out of all our afflictions.

DAY 7   *Daily bread. We are dependent on Him for our daily needs. The Holy Spirit. God gives the Holy Spirit to those who ask.

ANSWERS TO STUDY 3

PRAYER IN THE CHURCH RELEASES THE POWER OF GOD

DAY 1   They were to wait for the promise of the Father.
Jesus said they would be baptised with the Holy Spirit.
Share what members of the group have found in Acts 1:14 – reminding them that they – the early Christians – devoted, gave themselves, concentrated on prayer as a group.

DAY 2   God poured out His Holy Spirit on them all, filling them all. The Holy Spirit came, as promised, when Jesus was exalted to God's right hand.

DAY 3   *They prayed.
To devote themselves to prayer and to the ministry of the Word – preaching and teaching.

DAY 4   1) To enable them to speak with boldness. 2) For God to heal and do signs and wonders through the name of Jesus.
The Holy Spirit was poured out and they spoke with boldness – a specific answer to prayer.
Many signs and wonders were done by the apostles – the sick and people who had evil spirits were all healed.

DAY 5   With another miraculous escape from prison – a sign of God's power. The apostles began preaching at dawn with boldness. The two requests continued to be answered by the Lord.
Allow the group to share thoughts on '**NO PRAYER = NO POWER**'.

DAY 6   He laid violent hands on some of the Church, had James killed with the sword, Peter arrested.
Prayed earnestly.
Discuss God's answers to prayer recorded in verses 6-11.

DAY 7   *Praying.
*Amazed, unbelieving, etc.

ANSWERS TO STUDY 4

CHURCH LIFE AND GROWTH RESULT FROM PRAYER

DAY 1 Jesus is the Head of the Church. He is the one who is building it.
*Controls, directs, governs, co-ordinates.
It should be His right to direct, co-ordinate and control His body, the Church.

DAY 2 God the Holy Spirit spoke plainly to the Church. He told them to set aside two of their leaders for outreach.
Fasted, prayed, gave, laid hands on them, and sent them off – obeyed the directive.
Men praying.

DAY 3 Call to me, pray. He promises to answer and to reveal hidden things we do not know.
Encourage the memorisation of Jeremiah 33:3.
Allow the group to share their experiences.

DAY 4 Growth.
Word of God increased, disciples were greatly multiplied, many priests believed, Church was built up – strengthened in the faith, an increase in numbers, the Word of God prevailed mightily.

DAY 5 Encourage the group to realise that a healthy Church is a growing Church – in every way.

DAY 6 Allow students to share what they have written on James 4:2, and areas of need. These matters could be used later for group prayer. Note them.

DAY 7 He was always praying for the Romans, had not ceased to pray for the Colossians, prayed constantly for the Thessalonian church and for Timothy. He was a man of prayer – faithful, constant and consistent.

ANSWERS TO STUDY 5

PRAYER BRINGS VICTORY

DAY 1 Satan, the devil. He seeks to devour, defeat and destroy God's children.
*To pray at all times in the Spirit (v. 18) and be clothed in the protecting armour He has provided (vv. 13-17).

DAY 2 Pray at all times, in the Spirit, keep alert, persevere, pray for all the saints.
That we would not be taken out of this world, but be kept from the evil one.

DAY 3 *Ruler of this world, the devil, the god of this world.
The whole world is in Satan's power.
All the kingdoms of the world, all the authority and glory are Satan's, and he can give it to whom he chooses. Note that Jesus did not deny this.

DAY 4 Man is dead spiritually, sons of disobedience, following the prince of the air – Satan, they are children of wrath, dominated by passions and the flesh, in bondage. Slaves of Satan.
Jesus came to deliver us from the present evil age, to take away our sins, to destroy the works of the Devil, to destroy the Devil who has the power of death, and to deliver all who because of the fear of death had lifelong bondage.

The Devil would be cast out, utterly defeated through the victory of the Cross of Christ.

DAY 5 Jesus disarmed Satan's army, exposed it, and triumphed.
To lead us in triumph – victory – and to use us to spread the knowledge of Jesus.

DAY 6 Commands are: Submit to God; Resist the Devil; Draw near to God; Be free from sin. Promises are: Satan will flee from us; God will draw near.
Discuss practical steps to overcoming through prayer and faith.
On the basis that Jesus has already defeated Satan – see Romans 8:37.

DAY 7 *Be gone, Satan!
Authority to tread upon scorpions and serpents, and over all the power of the enemy – nothing shall hurt them.
*Resist him.

ANSWERS TO STUDY 6

BEGIN PRAYER WITH PRAISE

DAY 1   *Praise the Lord
The servants of the Lord, those that fear God, everything that breathes, the great and the lowly. If I'm a Christian, I'm included!

DAY 2   Spiritual sacrifices – gifts – offerings.
(1) The sacrifice of praise, the fruit of our lips. (2) Helping and sharing with others. God is pleased with these.

DAY 3   *The Lord.
*All that we are and have – totally.
*On ourselves.

DAY 4   His mighty deeds and His excellent greatness.
It is good and right and enjoyable to praise God.
He heals the broken-hearted and binds them up. He is in control of the stars.
God is abundant in power, we can't measure His understanding.

DAY 5   Allow the group to share their discoveries. Allow them to use these praises in the group prayer at the end of the class.

DAY 6   The righteous are to be jubilant with joy, singing to God – using instruments, shouting for joy, making a joyful noise to the Lord. So praise is to be spontaneous, joyful, musical, enthusiastic.
*Trumpets, lute, harp, timbrels, dance, strings and pipe, cymbals, new songs, loud shouts, raised hands.

DAY 7   Glorious praise. Share descriptions.
It is loud, hard to describe, voice of a multitude, like thunder, like rushing water, a glorious song of praise to the Lord.

ANSWERS TO STUDY 7

PRAYER IS THANKSGIVING AND CONFESSION

DAY 1   *An offering of thanksgiving. Come before Him with thanksgiving.
*Thanksgiving. (Look at Daniel 2:20-23).

DAY 2   Always. For everything. Not usually. Share other answers.
We are commanded to be thankful. Thankfulness is meant to be given to God – it is part of our worship, comes from a knowledge of the Word (v. 16). In all our living, giving thanks should be a part.

DAY 3   *God's hand is able to save – He is always listening. But if we persist in unconfessed sin, God's face is hidden and He does not hear our prayers – our fellowship with Him is broken.
A person with a clean life, with no deceit. James also tells us of our need for total cleansing – including within. Allow students to share their other answers.

DAY 4   *He knows all about it! Nothing is hidden. Because of sin in our lives God cannot hear our prayers. Even though we may be engaged in all kinds of religious activity (as in Isaiah 58:2-3), with sin in our lives there is a blockage in our prayers.
Confess my sin – own up to God, speak out about what I have done and receive His cleansing.

DAY 5   A sorrow for sin, godly grief that leads to repentance and turning away from the sin, brokenness and humility.
David's heart smote him. He had conviction of sin. He took the blame himself. I am responsible for every choice to sin in my life.

DAY 6   *God's own people.
Humble themselves. Pray. Seek God's face. Turn from sin.
*God will hear their prayer. Forgive their sin. Heal their land. God's eyes will be open to them.

DAY 7   *Daniel turned to the Lord, fasted, prayed and confessed the sins of God's people. He confessed the sins of all Israel, and his own sin.
*Rebellion. Disobedience. Rulers and people did not listen when God spoke through the prophets. Laws of God broken.
He began his supplication – asking God to do specific things.

ANSWERS TO STUDY 8

PRAYER IS INTERCESSION AND SUPPLICATION

DAY 1   *First place.
*All men, kings, all who are in high positions, leaders. Pray for peace, quiet, order, reverence towards God, with good behaviour.
The honour of the Lord, God's character, asked God to pardon the people because of His steadfast love, forgiveness for the people.

DAY 2   *God's people.
Asked God to hear his prayer; to restore the Temple in Jerusalem that was in ruins; to see the suffering of His people and the suffering of the city of Jerusalem; to forgive; to act and not delay. (Get the group to see that these were definite requests).

DAY 3   Share descriptions.
Someone to stand in the breach – an intercessor.
*Destruction and judgement.

DAY 4   It saved the nation from the judgement God had planned.
God does look for someone to stand in the breach, to save the land from destruction (Ezek. 22:30). Moses did so, and God spared the people.

DAY 5   Get the group to share their thoughts.

DAY 6   *THREE Loaves (A definite request).
With encouragement and promises – to ask and we will receive.

DAY 7   What do you want me to do for you?
He asked to be able to see again. (Get the group to see that it is good for our supplications to be definite also).

ANSWERS TO STUDY 9

CONDITIONS FOR PRAYER

DAY 1 *To abide in Jesus and His Words to abide in us.
*Walking closely with Jesus; enjoying His love and loving Him; learning what He is saying in Bible Reading and prayer; wanting to know and do His will.

DAY 2

THE TAX COLLECTOR	THE PHARISEE
He prayed to God, had nothing to say for himself. Prayed from a broken heart.	He prayed to himself. His prayer was full of 'I'.
He saw himself as he was before a Holy God – unworthy and sinful.	He was pleased with himself, anxious to convince God he was a fine fellow.
Probably felt unworthy as far as others are concerned. Stood afar off.	He despised others.
He went home justified.	His prayer had no effect.

God resists the proud, including their prayers, but gives grace and listens to the humble.

DAY 3 As Christians we should not aim to impress men, but to glorify God. In public places – synagogues and street corners. They were not concerned with coming to God in prayer, but wanted to be seen by men. They received no reward at all from God.

DAY 4 *They are selfish and pleasure-seeking.
*By not answering selfish prayers.
To glorify the Lord.

DAY 5 God forgives all my sin, does not repay in accordance with my sins, He removes them completely and forgets them altogether.
*Believe and forgive. So that we may be forgiven by God. It depends on my forgiving others. If I don't forgive, I am not forgiven by God.

DAY 6 It is total forgiveness: ANYTHING against ANYONE – no exceptions.
I AM TO FORGIVE AS GOD IN JESUS HAS FORGIVEN ME.

DAY 7 *It is our confidence. We may ask anything, and God hears us, if it is according to His will.
Jesus wanted to know and do the Father's will.

ANSWERS TO STUDY 10

MORE CONDITIONS FOR PRAYER

DAY 1   We need to pray in the Spirit.
The Spirit searches the depths of God; the Spirit knows the mind of God.
When we pray under His direction He can give us the mind of God and so we may pray according to His will.

DAY 2   A doubter is like the waves of the sea, tossed about, double-minded, unstable.
Doubt destroys our prayers. We receive nothing from God.
*We must have faith – even as small as a mustard seed. (Try to take some mustard seeds to the group for members to see and handle).
*Never to doubt.
Prayer can move immovable mountains and change impossible situations.

DAY 3   *To encourage us always to pray and not lose heart.
She is an example to us to keep persevering in prayer.

DAY 4   When we close our ears (and hearts!) to the cry of the poor and act meanly.
God gives lavishly – everything for our enjoyment. He wants us also to give generously.

DAY 5   *Jesus Himself.
To be people who belong to Him, submitted to Him, honouring Him as Lord.
*All to be in agreement.

DAY 6   A wrong marriage relationship will hinder effective prayer.
Unity of Spirit, sympathy, love of the brethren, a tender heart, a humble mind, blessing others.
The Lord sees the righteous and He is listening for their prayer.

DAY 7   To ask in Jesus' name.
Prayer is answered. God's will is done. God is glorified.

ANSWERS TO STUDY 11

TYPES OF PRAYER

Remember answers with an *do not require discussion time).

DAY 1   That children be taught diligently in the home, that the whole of life be permeated by His truth and relationship to Him.
*Personal.
Many answers. The family comes as a unit before the Lord in worship, to seek His help, direction, guidance and blessing.
*Personal.

DAY 2   Jesus says to do it! – privately, not with many words, but from the heart, out of total dependence upon Him. God rewards such prayer.
*Personal. Point out that daily prayer-time can be given to categories, i.e. nation, church, family, missions, friends, contacts etc.

DAY 3   Our usual thought is going without food. But see notes also. Jesus assumes we will fast – secretly, with no outward signs. God rewards this. Daniel fasted and prayed with confession and supplication. The Church leaders in Antioch were worshipping and fasting when the Holy Spirit spoke to them. They sent off the first missionaries with fasting and prayer. In Acts 14:23, there was fasting and prayer for the new elders. Jesus made it plain that His disciples would fast.

DAY 4   Share the contributions of the group.

DAY 5   *In answer to the King's question – 'What is it you want?' Nehemiah prayed and then spoke to the King.
Many answers – maybe – 'Lord, give me wisdom in my reply.'
They help me be aware that I have an all-day access to the Father, not just a set time.

DAY 6   Call the elders. Pray over him and anoint him with oil.
The Lord raises the sick ones and forgives their sin.
Confess our sins to one another and pray for one another.

DAY 7   Personal.
*Gifts of healing.
Personal.

ANSWERS TO STUDY 12

THE PRAYER LIFE OF JESUS

DAY 1 Jesus is our example – we are to follow in His steps.
He was submissive and obedient to God, reliant on Him and humble in spirit.

DAY 2 God always hears those who are living in obedience to Him
Jesus was the Beloved One, whose life pleased the Father.

DAY 3, DAY 4, DAY 5

Reference	Where Jesus prayed	When He prayed	The result
Luke 3:21-22	Jordan River	After baptism	Equipped by Spirit
Luke 6:12-14	Mountain	All night	Selected 12 disciples
Mark 1:32-35	Capernaum, alone	Long before dawn	Healing bodies and minds
Luke 5:15-16	Wilderness		Taught crowds
Matthew 14:9-23	Mountain, alone	Late afternoon	Taught and fed 5,000
Luke 9:28-31	Mountain with Peter, James, John		His glory was revealed
Luke 10:17, 21-22	Jesus gave thanks as He saw the 70 realising their spiritual authority		
Luke 11:1	A specific place	At disciples request	Taught them to pray
Luke 22:31-34	Passover meal	For Peter – that his faith would not fail	
Luke 22:39-46	Mount of Olives	Regular habit	Prepared for betrayal
Luke 23:34	On the cross	While he suffered	Prayed for OTHERS

DAY 6 The night of His arrest.
For the disciples, the believers. For believers down through history – us included (v. 20). He prayed: for the Son to be glorified; the Father to keep the followers of Jesus (vv. 11, 15); for His followers to be one (vv. 11, 21-23); for them to be sanctified; for His followers to be with Him.

DAY 7 In His earthly life, Jesus prayed with loud cries and tears and was heard because of His obedience.
Personal: but, we should note the following: At times when He was exhausted and busy, He made time to pray. He withdrew from successful ministry and much demand to pray. He had a custom to pray at all times of the day and night. I need to remember to do this in my own life. He is interceding for me.

THE WORD WORLDWIDE

We first heard of WORD WORLDWIDE over twenty years ago when Marie Dinnen, its founder, shared excitedly about the wonderful way ministry to a needy woman had exploded to touch many lives. It was great to see the Word of God being made central in the lives of thousands of men and women, then the life changing effects that resulted when they applied the Word into their circumstances. Over the years the vision for WORD WORLDWIDE has not dimmed in the hearts of those who are involved in this ministry. God is still at work through His Word and in today's self-seeking society, the Word is even more relevant to those who desire true meaning and purpose in life. WORD WORLDWIDE is a ministry of WEC International, an inter-denominational missionary society, whose sole purpose for existence is to see Christ known, loved and worshipped by all, particularly those who have yet to hear of His wonderful name. This ministry is a vital part of our work and we warmly recommend the WORD WORLDWIDE 'Geared for Growth' Bible studies to you. We know that as you study His Word you will be enriched in your personal walk with Christ. It is our hope that as you are blessed through these studies, you will find opportunities to help others find a personal relationship with Jesus. As a mission we would encourage you to work with us to make Christ known to the ends of the earth.

Stewart and Jean Moulds – British Directors, **WEC International**.

GEARED FOR GROWTH BIBLE STUDIES

You can obtain a full list of over
50 'Geared for Growth' studies
and
order online
at:
Our Website:
www.gearedforgrowth.co.uk

Further information can also be obtained from:
www.christianfocus.com

Find out more about WEC INTERNATIONAL at:
www.wec-int.org.uk or on Facebook